Table of Contents

Acknowledgements...........................1

Chapter 1: The Front Line...................11

Chapter 2: Small Beginnings...............19

Chapter 3: Embracing Change............34

Chapter 4: Destined for Greatness....48

Chapter 5: No Insignificant Move......58

Chapter 6: The Loss............................82

Chapter 7: Purpose Realized.............92

<u>Acknowledgements</u>

I want to thank my family for their support as I have endeavored to write this first book. I appreciate their support more than they will ever know.

To my wife, Jaclyn, who is my absolute best friend and partner in this life. I am so glad that our paths crossed and that we have been able to walk this road together. With all of the ups and downs that life has thrown at us, there is nobody else that I would rather take this journey with than you. Your class, support, and absolute commitment to our family is so appreciated.

To my beautiful and smart daughters, I hope you know that your dad loves you more than I can ever articulate or show in this lifetime. Each of you have a special place in my heart, and hopefully you will realize the intricate ways your lives will impact this world. Peyton, thank you for helping me by reading through the very first rough copies. Keep pursuing excellence in everything you do. Emma Grace, thank you for the laughs and being my shadow in getting things done. I hope you do not get tired of the music inclination you exhibit at this stage, the creativity you exude will help you pursue your dreams; dream BIG! Evelyn, oh my goodness, your zest for life and sweet nature is a blessing to our family. Praying that as you uncover the queen inside you that you will always know the pinnacle of success. Never second guess your value, and always be looking for those opportunities to impact those you meet. To all my family, know that there is one relationship more important than any other, and that is with our Lord and Savior Jesus Christ.

To my Parents, I appreciate all of your sacrifice and support throughout the years, and hope that you look at where my family and I are today and can smile with accomplishment; this has much to do with your support!

The cover was designed by my longtime friend and brother, Gabriel Lobsinger, I appreciate you taking all my thoughts and putting them into reality!

So, why this book? I have been talking for years about writing this. Why the press to do it now?

A couple reasons. First, I would like to be able to leave something behind that, by chance, my daughters could pick up and find some understanding of how their dad lived his life, even long after I'm gone. Second, I would like to think that perhaps there is someone that may find encouragement through reading this. Maybe I would be able to help someone struggling to find their way or their purpose in this life. We never know the impact we may have, and you will never be able to realize even the beginning of your purpose unless you are willing to put yourself out there for the world to see. My hope is that my best efforts will bring to fruition innate pinnacles in individuals whom I've met; that maybe there may be an effective way to do so via the written word. I hope it is a help to someone!

While this book may start off a bit slow to explain

a few terms and strategies, I can assure you that if you

continue on, you will find the strength and insight inside

the covers to accomplish its purpose for every pawn

who reads its contents.

Across the globe there are those who will always

be left standing alone, as the last in line from those

peers in a game in which everyone must participate. I

was lucky enough to have just enough athleticism to

typically not be afforded such an oftentimes

embarrassing moment in my adolescent years. Still, I

recall several times, shamefully, gliding sheepishly

behind a slower or less athletic classmate during a

dodgeball game or two. These kids, in our simple minds

at those ages, were definitely expendable. As the other team would approach the line to acquire the red rubber balls to begin the assault, making it apparent that those on the front lines were simply momentarily "shields" for our top guarded athletes. It wasn't until much later in life that I learned both the importance and the strategic hierarchy of those on the "front-line". Even in their inability to actually coordinate an attack against the other team, it is evident that even the weakest member on a dodgeball team still serves a purpose. Without them, the battle will never be won. While they cannot move as fast, jump as high, or perhaps throw as hard...they may offer some strategic advantage if they play their role properly. Where athletics may be far from them, perhaps they can understand another similar game of life comparing it to a less athletic concept:

chess.

In the game of chess there are several pieces on

the board that are set up in a specific way for the game

to begin. For the sake of anyone who may be reading

this book and is not familiar with these pieces I would

like to give a brief synopsis of them. In the second row

away from you, the player, you would place all of your

pawns side by side in the squares provided. The Rooks

(or Castle-looking pieces) go on each of your closest

corners. Next positioned alongside each of the Rooks are

the Knights (horse) pieces, then come your bishops on

subsequent positions to the knights (each should rest on

a different colored square), then your Queen (arguably

the most powerful piece on the board), and lastly the

King.

To further assist a reader who may be unfamiliar

with the game of chess, I find it necessary to quickly

explain the "layman's" insight on the moving strategies

for each piece. The Rooks are able to move in straight

lines as far as needed to accomplish attacks or defenses.

The Knights can move in a "L" shape of 2 up 1 over in

whichever direction is available. The bishops may stay

on their respective colored squares and move diagonally

in the directions. The King is able to move 1 space in any

direction. Finally, the Queen, in all her majestic wonder

can move any direction as far as she needs to,

accomplishing the will of the chess master. Yet nestled

directly in front of all these powerful pieces lies the Pawns, able to move forward two spaces on the first move, and 1 space after, only attacking when another piece is diagonal to it. You are familiar with the term Pawn. A pawn defined is the smallest valued piece on the board, however to a chess master who sees its potential is an intricate part of a greater plan. In the ultimate game, life, a pawn is often used to reference someone or something of little to no foreseen value. Only when the pawn painstakingly makes its way across the board through the thoughtful action of the Chess Master, is the true potential realized. The exchange happens instantaneously as the Pawn becomes the Queen. It's not always the most grandiose of transitions, there is little fanfare or epic moments; still the potential is there the entire time in obscurity. There are people

we encounter, moments we endure, and phases of life

that we traverse that will test our fortitude. My goal is to

expose those moments, to help point out the potential

for growth, and to inspire you to embrace the totality of

this life; both in its challenges and its times of ease. As

we embark on this thought, join me to explore the

Pawn's purpose.

<u>Chapter 1: The Front Line</u>

The front line. A line of insignificant pawns who are poised to begin the battle. Peering across the open space at the opponent's strength, preparing to engage at will. Seemingly without the proper power to actually invoke any real damage, and yet here, on the front line awaits the will of the Chess Master.

Whether it is a teen behind a counter, a host at a restaurant, the gas station attendant, the greeter at the grocery store, the sale professional at the local furniture store or dealership...often times there are underappreciated people who willingly stand on the front lines of society. I will say that as I am writing this book I am employed at a very incredible dealership as a sales manager, and I'm reminded every day of the blessing I have to be able to work with outstanding sales professionals. While we often, as managers, get the "kudos" for the successes, it is truly those who are engaging the guests at our facility that make the difference every day. I feel the need to express my current point of reference in my life, because this is a moment in which I am keyed up to notice "Pawns" in my life. Whether people whom I am trying to derive their greatest potential, or situations that leave me damaged, educated, or both.

Those who are able to stand in front line capacity and do so with the type of tenacity that it takes to make a company or team successful should be applauded. It could quite possibly be one of the most important and underappreciated places in the workforce. Those on the front line hold the key to daily success in their grasp. When developed they become insurmountable and impenetrable to failure. When handled incorrectly or unsupported, they will often wither away and be the demise of an organization. In the old fighting style of the military, it was the generals and officers that often were at the back of the line, and while I do not want to mitigate their importance; I in turn want to emphasize that if not for the front-line, battles would not be won.

It's the volunteers that go out to fight or those who decide that they want to work in the "trenches" of a company that truly make the wheels turn. While we need those of vision and poise, those of intellect and

ability to lead; we cannot think for a moment that those

with their hands in the mud and dirt "getting it done"

are of any less importance. Without those who are

willing to engage in front-line confrontations and

battles...wars would never be won.

When the COVID pandemic hit the shores of

America in 2020 my wife was considered "essential",

and therefore would never be given any sort of reprieve

from taking care of people's needs as the virus wrecked

the global economy. As an RN Supervisor at our local

hospital, she would report to work diligently every day.

As staff would need to quarantine throughout the

pandemic, she would cover shifts, take on more

workload, and do so with a tenacity not many can muster. She would cautiously go through her "after-work" routine to disinfect herself before coming home to 3 adoring children and me, as the doting husband. My kids and I, before I was shortly deemed "essential", would spend much of our days writing encouraging words on the sidewalk outside of our home. "Stick together, we will make it", "Our mom is a Front-line worker", "We love our RN", and the occasional encouraging scripture. It was our way of trying to spread hope of a better day; and when my wife walked into the house, dinner was ready. She was, after-all, a "front-line" worker, and exhausted from the stresses of the day. Still, I recall the day she asked us to all get into the truck after a long day of work to join her in the hospital parking lot. Our tight-knit community had organized an appreciation event outside our hospital. Many of the community filled the outside parking lot, and at one moment for several minutes began to honk horns, some clapped, and lifted joyous voice outside of their windows as nurses and doctors stepped outside. It was important that we acknowledged the fight they had engaged in, and to let them know that they were important.

It also made me wonder; how many times I had taken healthcare workers for granted? Still, now faced with a global pandemic, they stepped to the forefront where they had always been and began to glisten with value. Some who perhaps would have been considered simple pawns in the life we live, were there when we needed them. Still, the change had happened almost instantaneously before our eyes as they became the Queens of this game of life.

We had come to appreciate them. We cannot forget to appreciate and honor those in our lives who are on the front lines daily. Perhaps it's healthcare workers, police or firemen and women, teachers or counselors, pastors, or friends; those who are there, stalwart, and faithful to their call to be on the frontline. It's a noble calling to be in that position.

Frontline people tend to take the heat of the battle head on, if for no other reason than they realize that someone has to be there. Perhaps even with all of their seemingly lack of strength and obvious value...they are, in a sense, the most valuable of all. They are those

who creep ever so gingerly across a raging world,

perhaps in obscurity, never getting the credit they

deserve but forging ahead with unwavering faith in the

greater good of us all.

<u>Chapter 2: Small Beginnings</u>

The imagination of a child is a gift. The simplistic nature of what can be, coupled with the unadulterated faith of belief that it is attainable is unlike any other force on planet Earth. Children think with a type of carefree expression that leads to impervious thought not easily swayed by reality and logic. What happens? Why is it that we cannot seem to grasp firmly enough as we mature to that basic concept of faith?

Close your eyes, and imagine for a moment, as I attempt to take you back to where I grew up. The warm summer breeze whipping through the tops of a corn field. Feel the breath of nature blow through your hair as you look out across the golden tops of stalks. Smell fresh cut grass in the distance. Oil rigs creak as they

move up and down, and up and down. There is not a car

passing by, only the occasional songs of the robins and

jays echo as you're carried away to a world that you

imagine. As a young boy growing up, I did this often.

Riding my BMX bike that I had gotten for my birthday

and morphing it into my police issued motorcycle. I

would chase down the "bad guy" and need to catch a

flight across to the other side of the world on my

airplane; which looked eerily similar to my swing on my

playground set. I would land in a far-away country, now

as a federal agent. I always seemed to have connections

to weaponry that would assist me in accomplishing my

mission. To the cornfield I would go, like the jungles of

ancient countries that I had never been, but somehow

knew the exact layout of. Every place I went to would have a river that seemed to wind the same way that our creek did on the back side of our property. From early summer vacation until early fall on my way back to school, my days were filled with excitement and accomplishment.

It would boil over to hours, as most young boys of my day, playing with army men. I would come up with what seemed like millions of missions to accomplish. However, when the day was done, and the missions were complete or ended in devastating fashion; the next day all was well and there was a new set of missions to achieve. The imagination of a young boy was only limited by bath times, adult engagements, and bedtimes. I recall playing for hours at a time alone in a room, with nothing but GI Joe army men and my own methods of sound effects. While I can self-admit to having, possibly, an overactive imagination; I cannot think that I was too far removed from many other children my age.

As I am now grown and have a family of my own, I have enjoyed very much, watching my three daughters as they playout imaginary scenarios with their dolls. These are much different scenarios than what I enacted as a young boy, as mine were centered around saving the world, theirs are more placid and of a nurturing nature. I have been blessed with a wonderful wife who has exampled being a great mom to all of my girls, and so it's easy to see why they "play" mom the way they do. They are gentle, and attentive to every need of their baby. To all onlookers it is a sweet sight to see how they are so careful with what we see as a toy, but to them; it is a baby depending on their ability to provide care. We have been held up at events and outings as my middle daughter takes her time making sure the baby is changed, fed, and properly secured in the car before the ride can commence. I would have to admit that there have been times I have been a little frustrated with this whole process, but I must remind myself that this is as real to her as anything else at this stage of her life. In retrospect...she will most likely get a taste of similar interruptions from her little sister who loves whatever her older sisters do. Honestly, if we really put it into words, she is in a state of mind that most adults only wish to be back in. We have even gone as far as having birthday parties for some of her babies that she has gotten. Cupcakes, candles, streamers, and all of the party favors of a well-deserved party; because, if it matters to her, it matters to us.

Let no man despise thy youth... (1 Timothy 4:12)

There is something about a carefree way that children can play and imagine life. It's quite refreshing and even a bit alarming to think that we all were there at one point in time. Somehow, we seem to lose some of our creativity as we age. Where we dreamed of being an astronaut, we settle to be an accountant. Where some dreamed of performing on stage in front of millions, are now content to be in a cubicle in a high-rise in the middle of a company in a metropolis. Dreams were meant to be pursued, and yet at some point many just simply lose focus. We determine that instead of taking the risk of pursuing and failing, we play it safe and settle.

There are many successful people in the world today that in all definitions of the word, simply settled for less than what they were born for. They allowed themselves to tap a clasp in the mountain of life, tied a rope, and began building a city for themselves at far less than their peak. They begin to express their success not based on the potential they once dreamed about, but rather, from a perspective of acknowledging their position compared to others who they see on similar mountainsides.

Those who do not allow themselves to feebly drift into the lethargy of their existence, but rather press into the deepest caverns of their inner child seem to, often, be the success stories that we later write about. These few, followed, individuals allow themselves to dream child-like dreams and begin to enact them out in real-time. Their vision goes far beyond what they can see or obtain, and draws the attention of many who surround them, even if to look for a hope of a glimpse of the impossible for themselves. We see it in business tycoons, trainers, and many other success stories. What is it about them that would make them so special? I would challenge that the only difference is their assessment and ability to deal with the risk; coupled with an acute ability to see things that others will not or cannot. Still, even more so, the difference between a manager and a leader in a business field will always prove out in the way he or she challenges those around them to strive for their greatest potential.

I would confront you with the task of considering a pawn on the chess board. To an untrained and unlearned chess player, the potential of this small and seemingly insignificant piece in a grand gentlemen's game could be overlooked. Still, in the hands of a "Chess Master" he knows that he only needs to visualize the route for this piece to truly pull its possibilities out of its existence. While the path may be slow and cumbersome, the Master Chess player knows that if he can utilize the proper strategy, he can pull out the true powerful nature of the Pawn left in his care.

I would further press those true visionaries are not only successful people themselves, but they are able to acquire, identify, and empty into vessels the skills and talents that can sometimes not even be seen by such individuals that they lead. They pull out the intricate and powerful talents and abilities of those around them. They are those who can walk into a restaurant or a starter job, identify people who are only scratching the surface of their callings, and offer them a path to future success. They have learned how to identify diamonds in dirt hills.

There are so many things that challenge the imagination of a youth. A Pearl is formed when an irritant or foreign object moves into the oyster or clam and is not filtered. The mollusk will then develop a coating around it and continue to do so as a defense mechanism. The question could be asked of even us how we cope with irritants that flow into our lives. Do we embrace or filter out the irritants? You and I are much like this small inconsequential organism. If it did not embrace the irritation, would you or I know it? Of course, we wouldn't; and truthfully it would simply continue to exist, never having experienced the true treasure of what was available. Life is not so different for

an organism that dwells here in our cities and homes.

Some are not as grand and seem to be less significant

than another, but we are all surely woven together in a

tapestry that intersects each one to the other. There are

many cases where the irritant passes through without a

second thought of this oceanic organism, but then there

are special times where it cannot simply bypass the

situation. It must deal with it, and in doing so, by the

very nature that it does, it creates a priceless gem.

    Like the pearls that are formed out of irritation, it

is often those moments of struggle that we are

challenged with to either allow them to pass without a

second thought, or to glean from them some of life's

greatest lessons. To say that we should embrace trouble may cause you as a reader to put this book down and never pick it up again. So, rather than destroying your opportunity to grow, let me simply say that not every irritant is worth becoming a pearl, however, identifying the moments in which life may be serving you up a lesson.

The small minute moments of life that pass you by where you may not have given a second thought could be the opportunity for invaluable life lessons. Not every challenging moment will produce a pearl, however, if you never take the step to glean from life it's oftentimes undiscovered paths; you could miss a moment of deep insight. Understanding there may be more to the struggle is key to developing an appreciation for the "Pawn" moments in your life.

Be careful of the little things you allow to get in that are an irritant, but don't be afraid to embrace them as they could turn out to be of extreme value. There are situations that arise in our lives that often dictate a path that we must go, but what of those moments where we can choose? What we do in those moments of decision can often supply us with either treasure or deliver devastating blows. The moments of time in which each of us engage in our challenges are times to make the best or worst of our portion of moments. Every day is an opportunity to decide whether we will achieve the greatness we've dreamed of or settle for the simpler things; nothing worth having comes easy and yet many

things that come easy are not worth having.

Chapter 3: Embracing Change

So many faces adversity or challenges with a level of uncertainty. Or perhaps even disdain for the concept of giving up one's self-concluded identity, even if for the opportunity of something different or better. For instance, someone who has spent a mass portion of their life creating the persona of a business mogul who deeply enjoys the fine arts or outdoors. Locked inside the walls of an office, demanded to continue to wear the mask of a shrewd business tycoon with no feelings; however truly more in touch with a softer element than what they can ever show. Or it could be the case of a person's conclusion that they are simply at their peak, yet deep inside knowing there are more gears to take them to new heights. Still, to achieve those places would cause them to admit they have currently settled. We want people to simply accept us for what they see; however, I would venture to say that in most cases what you see is the smallest portion of what truly makes up an individual. I have met functioning alcoholics, functioning drug addicts, and functioning clinically depressed people who, even when they are in their own minds, are writhing in self-defeat and uncertainty. These are simply my thoughts from observation, and while I'm certainly not a doctor, I have found in most cases the people who adhere to "self-medicating" addictions do so to wrestle a sense of comfort from a deep pain in themselves. Finding precious moments of freedom from an otherwise stark reality. In many cases, reality is the most horrific concept to face.

The world and life, in general, are not all "rainbows and butterflies". It is oftentimes filled with disappointment, heartache, and despair. It is deranged and hard, and sometimes people feel better suited to not face it. They simply do not feel they are equipped to do so. They, therefore, turn themselves "inside themselves", and the cycle begins to reason with an already defeated self. The sense of self that fabricates a false belief: that they do not have the tools to make it. Many either resolve to live life in a fog of addiction and defeatism or simply choose to "check-out" to the absolute chagrin of those who love them dearly; people who fought desperately to convince said individual of their love for them.

Change is difficult. In breaking unhealthy habits and cycles, one must employ, oftentimes, extreme measures. One comedian said, "to eat healthy you just have to trade all the good and tasty stuff for the disgusting unwanted stuff". While that seems often to be the general consensus, if that is how we try to tackle changing life, it is a good explanation for why so many struggle. If you are only looking at it from a singularly negative point of view and not establishing the achievements and goals that will benefit you overall, then it stands to reason why you may fail.

Take, for instance, the alcoholic. There is more than likely a reason they have chosen to drink themselves to a place of addiction. Perhaps they feel like they are out of control of their life and for that brief time in which they are intoxicated, they can simply forget about the unfairness of life. However, we know the effects of alcohol on the body will only further drive them to hardship later in life, should they make it to a well-seasoned age. Therefore, the heights they were meant to reach may never be realized, simply because they have chosen a path that will cut their existence on this earth short. Herein lies the dilemma: how can one overcome their vision of their reality and see further toward their utmost potential?

Being able to embrace change takes an individual tapping into his or her innermost being to understand his or her purpose. Once you understand your purpose, you can begin to see past anything that would derail your focus. I know that I am supposed to help people. That is what my passion is - encouraging the BEST out of people. This includes my family. My way may be different than yours; as I am a preacher and consider myself a "God-fearing" man. Therefore, I pray, I ask for guidance, I read, I meditate, and I look for opportunities to be there for people with whom my life intersects. It is why I am writing this book. In hopes that perhaps someone reading this may find some resolve to continue on another day. Someone who feels they are simply a Pawn in the game of life.

As a teen I felt very discouraged. I could not tell you the date, but I can tell you it was a Wednesday evening that I decided to end my life. As I was raised in a very religious home, I knew some of my actions would not bring any good towards my family name. I allowed anger to infiltrate into my being, and every time my dad left for work, I would need to "man-up" and take care of the house. This did not come from any parental pressure, but I took it on, internally, to toughen myself up. I recall, regrettably, several times yelling at my dad as he would leave to go to work, "You don't even love us"! As a truck driver whose terminal was over two hours from our home, I can only imagine how hard his drives were at times, especially now that I have a family of my own and put some incredibly long hours in. Still, he did what he needed to do to provide as good of a life for us as he could. We were never without food or necessities, and quite frankly, we had whatever most kids wanted. Most of my childhood was spent in a trailer house that was on my grandparents' property, and in my early years I had very fond memories of growing up so close to family. My aunt's and uncle's house were just on the other side of my grandparents', and so my cousins and I would play quite frequently. While my family connection brought an immense strength and bond, it also did not shield me from the challenges of the world completely.

I spent much of my younger years defending myself, and trying to fit in. I was never in the "really poor kid" category, but I was definitely out of place with the "in" crowd. Quite honestly, even now I struggle with higher up type "A" people. I have just grown up to where I do not care what most people think of me. As a teen, however, I had finally reached that point of giving up on life. It didn't seem fair that my dad worked as hard as he did, and I never really got to see him; yet we could not seem to get ahead. The stigma of our financial situation was so extreme that when I got the mail one day after school, I was furious with my mom. There was a piece of mail that said "... Welfare ...."; which I later learned was not what I thought. I was determined to quit school and get a job right then and there. In my mind we were a sub-middle-class family who were barely scraping by, and yet, I was missing all the time that my friends described with their dads being home. I did not fit in. Much of what I was doing outside the church house we attended would have been frowned on, and yet my mom had instilled principles into my makeup that would not allow me to dabble quite as deep as some in the less comely things of society. Consequently, my way out was going to be a night alone, with dad working and the rest of the family gone, and a loaded pistol.

Thankfully this was not my life-plan as orchestrated by God. He would offer me a moment, an encounter with him one night during a mid-week church service. It was a Wednesday night Bible study, and I could not even tell you what was preached, because I was mad that I was there. However, I can recall that when the altar call happened, I was a stone statue in my seat. I refused to move. So God sent someone to move me. The preacher walked directly down the side isle of our small church and looked directly at me and said, "Young man, what you are planning to do tonight is NOT God's will for your life. Since you didn't move when I opened the altar, God sent me back here to you. He wants to take all your anger, hurt, and frustration and use it to reach people. He wants you to give it to him tonight. You're not a loser and everything you're facing you will defeat...YOU WILL WIN."

As tears rolled down my cheeks, I thought to myself, "If an eternal God can step into a moment of time for a kid like me, to reach for me...then I have to see what my life can bring". It was shortly after that God called me to preach and gave me a scripture at the altar: 1 Peter 5:6, "Humble yourselves therefore under the mighty hand of God, that he may exalt you in due time." I did not know the impact that this one scripture would have on my life; but I was about to.

God was trying to help me embrace changes I would have to make to achieve the things He would have for me to achieve. He began dealing with me about the game of chess, hence this book, and revealed to me the concept of a PAWN. A seemingly insignificant piece in the hands of an untrained or perhaps rookie chess player, in the hands of a chess-master, the pawn is packed with potential for greatness. The limits exist for

the pawn's abilities to move, and often the movement

does not seem as great and significant as the other

pieces on the board. Still, inside the makeup of this

game piece, as it stumbles its way across the board;

carrying inside itself the glimmer of greatness. While the

war rages around it, and the battle ensues, in its

unwavering determination, it finds itself on the opposite

side of which it began. At this climactic moment, the

chess-master simply reveals the power inside this

inconsequential piece, as he reveals it as a QUEEN. The

journey may have been long; it may have had some

stalls and fumbles, but slowly and steadily its purpose

becomes revealed; as it becomes the most powerful

piece on the board. Whereas before, it could only move

single spaces and attack opportunistically, it can be now unleashed to move as far in whichever direction is deemed appropriate by the hand and mind of the chess-master.

All in a flickering moment the Pawn reaches its predetermined goal as deemed by the Chess Master. Whereas it was limited just a moment before, now it is able to move in seemingly limitless fashion. Do not fight the journey. Rather, embrace the change. Don't curse the smallest of progressions, rather, focus on the designated end that has been purposed for you alone; and in doing so, you will find the Pawn's Purpose.

Chapter 4: Destined For Greatness

Every day we walk by greatness. Seldom do we understand or truly see it for what it is, because it's often wrapped in the illusion of the mundane and mediocre. It's the kid who is misunderstood, or the old man with the veteran hat on his head, or your co-worker with dreams that they've never shared; but greatness is all around us in this world. Locked up in mankind is the very nature to dominate and to create something bigger than himself. Yet, all too often, it is a fleeting thought that is passed by without a second glance.

I remember as a child the awe-striking nature of Christmas morning. I would barely sleep, which made it difficult for the gifts to make it under the tree, with the

Ole St. Nick illusion still alive and well. I would inevitably have to wait until some of our other family would arrive that morning before tearing into gifts. Then would ensue the "guess what's in the package" pressure of having to make assumptions based on weight and form through the package. The excitement would almost kill my little heart as I would guess, most times not having a clue of what was inside those beautifully wrapped packages. It would be reaffirmed over and over, "I don't think that's what's in there, you have to guess again…", but I just wanted to open them up. I wanted to see what was inside the package!

This is the same concept with people. Some wrapped, perhaps, more beautifully than others, but there are an unimaginable assortment of skills,

concepts, and passions inside them. There are dreams,

goals, and achievements waiting to be unveiled. How

many times do we simply walk by them, and not pull

back the façade to truly see what is on the inside of a

person? In the segmented world in which we live we

encounter individuals, oftentimes for only a moment, in

which we generate a theory on their person based on a

few minor interactions. It is due to these small moments

of time that we often are subject to improper

judgements based on our limited knowledge of the

person, and more systemically derive conclusions based

on our past experiences.

I spent many years as a minister in the local jail where I resided. The biggest distinguishing point between myself and the men I ministered to was that I was able to go home at the end of my evening. Life had happened. There were choices that were made. Some were habitual offenders that, through poor decision-making abilities, seemed to always find themselves on the "wrong side" of the outcome. However, in my tenure at this facility there were always those individuals who just did not fit. There were those who I could tell were in this place because of a bad moment. One such individual captured my attention on a Monday evening when class was just getting ready to commence. When he walked into the room, he was joyful, and his smile told a story of a young man who had a bad moment. He was making the best out of the outcome, but he had

more inside of him than what he had thus uncovered.

I promptly broke protocol and offered him my

contact information and told him that upon his release I

would do my best to help him get his feet under him. I

told him I felt God had a plan for his life, and I meant

what I said. He went to a Federal Prison to serve the

remainder of his sentence. I made sure to write to him,

but I never received a letter in return. It was years later,

after I had ceased the program at the local jail, that I

met this man, through fate, outside of the brick and

mortar of that small room. I reminded him of one

concept that he heard me often discuss: Life is moments

- a lot of small individual moments in which a person can

choose how they will advance or retreat from their calling. Just because one moment did not work out how you feel it should have, does not mean that your entire existence is worthless. This young man for years struggled with life; however, every time life struck him...he got back up. It did not matter how many obstacles or how many circumstances. I recall being able to be there for him throughout his life for several years, doing my best to simply be a friend and to help him. He continues to get back up, and I am glad to say that I have confidence he has overcome his "moment" that tried to determine his life's course. I proudly call him a friend. He refused to succumb to what fate would seemingly deal his hand to play. I'm confident to tell you that his greatness, as I write this, is still yet to be determined.

Greatness or Success is defined differently by each individual. I recall moments in my teenage years, being fairly musically inclined, identifying my success as signing a record deal, and being able to perform in front of massive crowds of people. I had been locally successful with music and had become a viable option for music in the local church I attended. Still, there came a day in which maturity hit me and my definition of success altered. I saw how my dad worked over the road as a truck driver to provide for his family. I saw how he treated my mom. While most people's marriages were at about a fifty percent success rate with them living together, somehow my parents thrived and provided us with a very stable home despite demanding career choices. There were times in which my adolescence got the better of me, and my dad had to make the almost 3-hour drive back to work with the words, "...you don't even love us, you always leave..." in his mind. Yet, he strove to provide us the best way he could, and to give us a better life. He continued to make the drive, so that we would not have to leave our family and friends that we had grown accustomed to having around.

At some point, my "switch flipped" on my definition of success and greatness. I began pursuing characteristics in myself that would help me be the best Husband I could be, to be the best Father I could be, to be the best Employee I could be; and, essentially, to be the best person I could be. While I do not profess to have attained any of this, I can say that it is a daily mission of mine to pursue those callings. Greatness will be defined differently to every individual and measured by many varying and often inconceivable standards to the masses. To ascertain truly what it is to have succeeded or to have grasped even the hem of greatness; too many times it comes after a person's life is extinguished. Perhaps this is the reason for a hopeful author like me: to have written this book, so after I am gone from this world perhaps someone may find solace in my writings.

There are many who have left this world, and their greatness was never acknowledged, and perhaps they never realized the difference they made. I implore you to make certain that those individuals whom you can identify impacted your life. Expound to them that

they have made a difference. That could be the single-

most important gift you give someone is to let them

know they are seen as valuable and meaningful in this

life. Understand we all begin this life on the same path:

destined for greatness.

<u>Chapter 5: No Insignificant Move</u>

Faith. It's a challenge of the very logic and impulse that we work so hard to attain throughout our adolescence. It's the thing we lose as we get older, or at least it becomes more challenging. As toddlers we will leap through thin air toward the open arms of a loved one, with no doubt at all that this brief moment of seclusion and impulsion will not end in anything other than jovial bliss. It is why as teenagers you will get on the most insane and adrenaline driven rollercoaster, and then oftentimes are left holding the coats at the end of the line in your 40's. Somewhere in the quest for logic and careful consideration many lose the ability to believe in something that is not tangibly there or safe.

"I'm going to leave the car business." That's what I said

to my Pastor. My career was taking off, and for seven to

eight long years I had ground out a clientele that was

loyal, kind to me, and knew almost as much about my

family as anyone else I had ever met. They all got the

letters as my wife, and I worked through life's ups and

downs. They knew my major life events every quarter as

I worked desperately to connect for the sake of a

paycheck. People buy from who they "Know-Like-and

Trust"; so, make yourself a part of their family. That's

what I was good at, and I did it in a genuine way. I *did*

care about their kids, and their problems, and their

vacations and life events. However, sitting around a

dinner table one night, getting ready to head back to the

dealership, I remember those heart-shattering words

from my wife: "I did not get married to be alone." It

ECHOED as I finished dinner, gave my daughter a kiss

and walked out to my car, heading back to prepare for

the next day's events. I was successful. I was paying cash

for most of her college and provided a good quality of

life for my family.

Days went by and I received a call from my dad

who wanted to talk. I barely had time to get the call,

because I was providing for my family, and, boy, Dad

should be proud. However, on the other end of the line

was a voice that most of the time would struggle to find

words. "Son, I know you are successful and doing

good...but don't do what I did to you kids. You're missing

your daughter growing up...make sure you put God first, then your family, and then your job..."

I hung the phone up a bit disgruntled that everyone I was working so hard to provide for or impress seemed like they were not appreciating what I was doing. Most of my days seemed to fly by as I engulfed myself in car deals, training the new guys, going to the after-work events to represent my company.

Then came the evangelist. He was one of those guys that seemed to know everyone's business in the church. What a spiritual powerhouse he was! People got nervous because, while he was preaching, he would just stop, and bend down...ask permission of the people to open up dialogue; then call your number out. He would say things that nobody else knew, and you could tell because of the reactions of people. Lives were being changed and touched that night. Impacts that would stretch even now as I type this chapter. It was time for God to be direct with me. One night during the revival weekend, as I was praying at the altar and asking God for direction on what I was supposed to do; here came the preacher. He stopped me from praying and looked me right in my eyes and asked me, "Where is your ministry?"

Not knowing what he was asking I cordially let him know this was my home church, and I ministered here.

He asked me, "What do you do for a living, are you in sales?"

Well sir, you hit the nail on the head, and you have my attention. He began to call me out on letting my ministry go stagnant and ineffective while I chased my career, and if I was going to get what God promised me, I would have to realign my priorities. Let me tell you what that meant in short form. A six-figure job quickly became a 25,000 per year job, but bills were paid, food was bought, and I still can't tell you how; BUT GOD.

No move is insignificant. During my time away from the car business I enveloped myself in reconnecting with my God and my family. In doing so, I found a new appreciation for the ministry that God called me to by reaching the broken and lost souls of this

world. I took a temporary job at a chemical company

and found myself surrounded by people who I could talk

to and show God's love. The work was less stressful, and

so I began to listen to preaching while I worked. I could

feel myself gaining spiritual strength as the weeks

became months, and months became years...prayers for

discernment became the normal interjections again. I

would never know why God would ask me to do what he

did, but I was soon to find out.

My very good friend burst into my house one

evening, enraged, and gripping a cell phone in his hand.

Once we began to talk, I fought the urge to join with his

thought processes. His daughter was texting a boy who

had convinced her to sneak out of the house and leave

with him. The plan seemed so Romeo and Juliet, but if

you're a father and reading this; you know the feeling.

This was not a good situation. You must know that this

girl was called and accepted the call to the Mission Field

prior to this happening. Yet here, on a seemingly very

vivid chess board, this pawn was looking to be removed.

Whether it was a deferred hope that she felt delayed

her global involvement, or some other reasoning that

was detaining her goal to minister globally we may never

know. Still, whatever the reason; I found myself in a

spiritually high alert state.

Soon after I had heard the news, my friend and his

wife confronted their daughter (we all know how that

went). I finally reached out to her and reached into every class I had taught her, and every time I prayed with her at an altar. I asked her to do me a favor, if I was any sort of spiritual authority in her life, to give me one week of prayer; just one hour per day. I would not wish this type of feeling on anyone when it comes to someone they care about. I had seen her grow from a 7-year-old little girl to a 17-year-old adolescent, and about to make a very costly mistake with the wrong misguided agenda. I took one hour every day after I finished my shift at the chemical company and went by the church to find a spot in our prayer room to pray for guidance and that God would step in. I pleaded with God to please answer and while she had committed to the same schedule of prayer, that God would speak through the noise and remind her of His plan for her life. It wasn't day 1 or day 2 that brought any solace, but by Day 3 God answered and I received a call from this young lady stating that she had heard from God. I am pleased to report that she did end up preaching the Gospel on foreign soil. God is a fantastic chess master, and no move is insignificant.

Another day at the Chemical Company left me in absolute awe. As I had transferred from one team to another I was welcomed into the new team with, "You're that preacher, aren't you?"; I replied with a hearty, "Guilty as charged!"

Apparently, I had spoken to enough of my former colleagues about my passion for my relationship with

Christ, that it had gone further than I had thought it would. It was not necessarily always a welcomed part of my life by those who maybe did not follow my zeal, if at all. Therefore, it was no surprise when the next piece of the conversation was a very sharp, "There's no preaching allowed in the pod..." With my resolve of the sense that God had led me to this place for this time, I simply replied, "I will not preach until you ask me to" with a smile that most would have assumed I was being sarcastic. However, I truly endeavored to make myself available to anything that God would try to do in or through my life. For the next few months, I spent time assisting the team where I could, making small talk, and generally trying to have some fun while accomplishing what we needed to on a day-to-day basis. Not too long after arriving there (months down the road) I began

talking to this lady, who had so aptly asked me not to

preach while at work, about her son who was falling

alarmingly behind on his weight gain. The conversations

typically involved some facts along with making jests

back and forth about feeding the infant buttered

noodles to fatten him up. Obviously, we were in a

position in which she felt comfortable enough to open

up her very real situation to me; we had become friends

after all. I recall the day though where she began to tell

me that they were preparing to set an appointment with

a very prominent hospital to potentially do a procedure

on a nodule that they had discovered on his esophagus.

All at once I pulled open my Bible app on my phone and

turned to the scripture in the book of James in which it

speaks of calling on the elders to lay hands on the sick and they SHALL recover. I slid the phone over to her portion of the desk with that verse highlighted in bright yellow. Her response was, "What's that?"

"It's the Bible." I said, with a bit of a smirk on my face. To which she promptly explained that the religion that she was "does not do that"; in response I let her know that nobody except for GOD can do anything anyway. I asked her if I could come to pray with her son, because I had the faith to believe God for a miraculous healing. I would like to tell you that I was invited over that evening to pray and that in any desperate situation that involves a child; the parents would try almost anything to save them from pain. However, it did not go that way.

Instead, she emphatically declared that her religion "did not do that stuff".

I replied in jest, "Good thing God cares less about religion and more about what He said he would do." She did not think that was humorous.

I will tell you that another acquaintance from another team had been walking by our team's area while we talked about the scripture I referenced, and she decided to ask for help for her situation.

She too did not necessarily go to a church in which they believed God for healing and the miraculous, however, she was intrigued that I whole heartedly DID believe it. She let me know that her Father was sick and needed prayer and asked if I would come pray for him. Now, before I get too far ahead, I will tell you that I was

grateful that she asked me; so much that before I asked

what was wrong, I said, "No problem, I would love to".

She then proceeded to explain to me the hospital ICU

that her dad was in, and that his organs were shutting

down. He needed a procedure on his heart; however, he

was too weak to get it done. The doctors were not

offering her a lot of hope, and basically had left her to

simply watch her dad pass away in a frail state of affairs.

When I got off work, I went to the church to get some

anointing oil, and if I can be transparent enough to pray

and ask God to intervene at some point. This is where

some become very philosophical with their prayers. I did

not have time nor the eloquence to make God swoon

over my limited vocabulary. I simply said, "God, you're

up...I cannot do a thing in this situation..." and began

praying all the way to the hospital. As I pulled into the

clergy parking of the hospital I got out of my car in my

jeans and polo shirt I had been wearing all day, and

thought, "This will end up being the most unorthodox

miracle this family may ever see...", and I went inside.

You must understand the undertone of what I'm

trying to help someone with who may be reading this

book. I looked like a pawn, insignificant, and not in

typical ministerial garb...however, the mission I was on,

and the "marching orders" I was following had nothing

to do with me; and all to do with the One controlling the

pieces.

As I got near to his room, I found my co-worker in the hall. She greeted me with a smile and led me inside the room where her father was. The machines were pumping, beeping, and overall keeping everything in order. I recall he was in the bed closest to the window, and in this particular instance, was in a double room. I smiled at the patient next to him and peered around the curtain that had been pulled for privacy. He had a very warm sense about him as he lifted his head slightly off the pillow to greet me with a smile, "You're the preacher?". I apologized for my attire but explained that I don't think God is too concerned with that for now. After speaking for what seemed like mere moments, I asked him if he believed that God could heal him. He replied that he did, so I followed that up by asking his daughter the same question; to which she responded likewise. Again, no grand speeches, no pomp and circumstance; simply a pawn in place for the chess master to move against disease and sickness.

The following day. to the alarm of his daughter, he was rushed to the well-known hospital with indication he would be in a 4-day medically induced coma. At the risk of sounding like a spiritual boaster, I promptly explained to her that he would be awake the next day; and instructed her to tell her father that "...all glory goes to God". It happened as I said it would and she called me amazed when he began walking within twenty-four hours of his procedure.

I am happy to report that this gentleman lived a good while after God had healed his body. I am also happy to write that the report of the healing reached the ears of my fellow co-worker who had turned down the same opportunity. I do not write these few moments in which I've been privileged to see some incredible things transpire to boast, rather I write them to let you know that no move is insignificant.

After a couple years out of the car business, in an attempt to try to provide a better living for my family, I embarked on yet another potentially lucrative business venture. As an outside sales representative doing business to business sales, I will tell you that I may have scratched the surface on a more dreadful profession, and hated person, than a car sales professional. I won't bore you with the details of the grind of this position, but I will recount the day that I was on my way to another potential sale when everything came to a sudden halt; literally. I was involved in a motor vehicle accident, and it was my fault. My car was totaled, and we were not in the position to replace or repair it. Remembering the "good old days" of having money to burn I remember thinking, "What now?" as I towed the vehicle to my parent's house for the time being. Little did I know my next move was being planned.

I began searching for a vehicle to replace my one that I had wrecked, and it led me to a dealership that I knew one of the sales guys. It wasn't long until the General

Sales Manager approached me in the showroom and asked, "Are you 'JB'?" He and I talked for a moment, as he began to offer me a position, knowing who I was and that I had a career previously with a competitor. I originally turned him down, but he insisted that I take a look at what he would offer me to rejoin the ranks of the Automotive Sales Professionals. After speaking to my wife, my Pastor, and my parents...along with some time in prayer; I decided that I would take him up on the offer with the understanding that I would have a focus on GOD, FAMILY, and then WORK. Shortly after I began working at this dealership, I found myself going to lunch one day. I was on a bit of a health kick, and so I had decided to stay with a sandwich chain that offered fresh ingredients and salads versus the typical greasy spoon type of other facilities. However, on this day the Master of Moves had other plans as he began impressing on me that the "south of the border" fast food seemed like a much better option for today. As I walked in to get in line I looked up and saw a sight for sore eyes. It was my friend that I had met inside the confines of the jail walls from years ago, and the reconnection had now taken place. As I entered the restaurant I was greeted with a hearty, "JB"!

I began to clown him about not calling me or writing me back, but he promptly revealed from his back pocket the note I had sent him. This moment was a pivotal moment in both of our lives. He was given a help and a support that quickly became a family tie, and I received the confirmation of purpose for why I still was on the path I walked.

When you develop the ability to contour your thoughts and ideologies around the flow of the better way for your life, you will find satisfaction in every opportunity. I have saturated my thoughts and desires after things that are greater than me, and in doing so; I find that I conduct myself with purpose in the process of every move made. NO MOVE IS INSIGNIFICANT; it's up to us to find the reason.

Many people live their lives on a day-to-day impulsive nature; meaning they do not live on purpose. Rather, I would suggest that many in society today simply exist day-to-day and are not, in a sense, really living. In dealing with the issue of movement in life in respect to

movement in the game of chess, each piece has several

opportunities for movement. However, simply because a

pawn could be moved to a certain spot in play, doesn't

mean that every spot lends itself to the most

advantageous positioning for the well-being of the pawn

or the endgame to be success. Plan your moves

accordingly, with purpose, and prayerfully to determine

not a possible move, but rather the right move.

Chapter 6: The Loss

How you respond to loss is almost as important, if not more so, as the response to victory. Anyone can embrace good news. Very few people will struggle to simply grasp the positive points of life that may befall them. It has been wondered why some who have had such vigor toward a particular path in their life can suddenly take a step down a steep sloped hill that seemingly derails the potential they were once so close to achieving.

As we have explored the viewpoint of a Pawn from a position of individuals; I would like to take a moment to explore another variation of the same concept. Perhaps in a way to help some readers elevate their state of mind, to reinvest in the potential goal of accomplishment. If you are reading this book, then a simple message is that it is not too late for you. Simply, the fact that you are inhaling and exhaling oxygen and coherently breezing through the pages of this written word tells me there is still more for you to do. No matter your state of life, no matter your socioeconomic status, no matter your current dilemma or storm; you still have purpose.

It is the minor events that happen in an individual's life that can oftentimes nudge toward or deviate from the ultimate purpose of their life. A decision to go when you could have learned an invaluable lesson in staying, or just the opposite can be true, yet in either instance it is important to balance the risks and rewards of life's choices. We've heard the expression about hindsight being 20/20, but what if we could discipline ourselves to think ahead in those moments? Play chess, and not checkers, so to speak. This is a learned philosophy of life, I believe, that is often developed in the fires of trial and error.

We all risk every day. Most very successful entrepreneurs are accomplished because they are able to assess risk and balance it against the potential for reward. Success is never guaranteed, but as the saying goes, "Nothing ventured, nothing gained". Many of the sales professionals I have had the pleasure of training and working with over my career in the automotive industry have heard me say a time or two, "Play chess and not checkers" as a way of reminding them that we must plan our days, or our days will always have their way with us. The very essence of going to a job of any sort is us taking the position that our time used to accomplish the task is worth the reward or paycheck at the end of the week or month. When the effort required to accomplish the task seems to not be a valid reward for what it takes to do so; people's contentment curve begins to wane. We are, daily, trading a commodity in which we are unable to replenish (time) for a reward that there will seemingly never be enough of (money). So, what you do to assess your successes in this life is important.

To bring another object lesson, of sorts, into play for a moment. A good gardener knows the proper way to grow plants is to assess from the main stem, amidst perhaps the multitude of fruits that will grow from a main branch; the best of the bunch. The gardener will then, much like a chess master, prune away the "leach" fruits to better provide sustenance to the fruit that is already making headway in growing. This is all done in an effort to allow the fruit that has been chosen to grow larger and more robust. Just because there seems to have been a pruning in your life, perhaps a relationship, job, or moment, doesn't mean your ultimate well-being is not taken into consideration. We must learn, as maturing individuals, to evaluate each "pruning" in our life, to see how it will best benefit us towards our success. This involves taking emotion out of the scenario, and simply being in the moment; resolute and steadfast. Being focused on what the main purpose is for your life and not deviating from what you know to be true simply because of a moment of discomfort.

It is not realistic to believe that in the game of chess you will have no loss of game pieces, just as it is not rational to assume that one will never encounter loss in life. When dealing with an individual's losses, for instance a career change, a relationship change, or what have you, it's important that a person can assess logically the position that it leaves them in overall. This is best done without the cumbersome and often reckless burden of emotion. Not to say that emotion will never or should never play a role, but for a space of time one should take a step back and assess logically.

I'm reminded of a situation I watched play out in real time in which a family was dissolved. I'm not here to get into semantics of rights and wrongs, but from my purview I watched a mother handle the situation with zero regard to how it would affect her children. From one marriage to another within months, possibly due to the extra relationship she had formed while still married. In either regard, it was the kids that I watched suffer most of the hardship while their world was torn apart, and in the moment of their life where they desperately needed security and assurance from their parents (yes BOTH of them) they were left wondering. Every move in life has consequences. Even sometimes when we do not feel the brunt of the blow, we must be cautious in those times where life is throwing brutal blows to our stability, or sometimes it can do irreparable damage to important pieces of our lives as a whole. This individual used zero logic in her decision making, and almost one hundred percent emotional and self-centered life altering decisioning. Much of her reasoning was what she felt there were immoral tendencies of her previous husband, but in taking a step out to develop a relationship prior to ending her marriage; her morality was dashed.

Secondly, there was the loss of physical attraction, and yet ended up married to the second party who was in the same physical shape as the first.

The third point of reasoning given was the lack of help and mobility, and yet again the second individual she decided to be with is no more physically able than the first. Instead, her children now have to navigate a blended family, with an overbearing man who asserts himself as their ultimate authority figure in a demeaning way. This is just one of many stories in our society that breaks my heart, because quite honestly marriages are often ended or saved on simple and sometimes uneventful daily decisions to cultivate love in the home.

Still, the entire point of bringing in this particular situation is to help explore the real understanding that the small moments and decisions we make can impact even more than our own fates and ideas. It is important that we realize the long-term effects of our decisions, and when loss is inevitable to check our emotions. Engaging our logic and giving time a chance to clear the clouds that would blind us from regaining our bearings before we continue forward is what can determine a simple mistake from a chain-reaction of missteps. It has been widely accepted as humor to watch a stumbling individual slip on a banana peel or get caught up in a trip. However, in life there are real consequences to those moments.

Chapter 7: Purpose Realized

As the final chapter of this small and hopefully inspiring book comes to a close, I hope that it has filled your heart with the smallest inclination to drive you to your purpose. The most fulfilling thing for my life would be that I could perhaps help someone along the way, and that each individual I encounter will hopefully leave ever so slightly better having met me. I hope that the words written here have been a help and inspire your dreams to live again louder and more vivid than before. All we can really do is be good human beings to one another and treat each other with love and respect. All of our gadgets and things will fade, but the mark you leave on an individual's soul is forever; we often do not realize this until it's too late. So, with that, I hope you enjoy this final chapter.

What do you do when you've spent your entire existence in obscurity and finally find your purpose? Do you simply move on to fulfill that destined promise of successes and trample through the final play of your existence in a self-fulfilling haze? I hope, by this point of the book, you know that my thought on the matter would promote a much different response. However, I would say that even as the Pawn on a chess board reaches the intended goal through the guided hand of the chess master and becomes a Queen; it does not simply negate the ongoing battle. There are others crossing the same board it just embarked on and won.

So, with newfound rules of engagement for itself and

new abilities to move; turns itself back toward assisting

in the win for others.

The amazing thing about life is that until the final

breath is taken you are able to make a difference. The

true testament and power of one's life lies directly in the

hands of that sole-person based on daily choices. You

may say, "...but I cannot reach or affect as many as this

or that individual", and you may be correct. However,

your purpose may be for a different set of people, or

perhaps maybe just that ONE individual. Remember,

never diminish the power of a single, seemingly

insignificant, soul. The world is full of catalyst-type

people, who, upon finding the strength to achieve their

purpose, changed the world. We may never truly understand the impact we have on those we've been in contact with. Still, if we live every day understanding our own purpose and staying focused on why we are still here among the living, I have reason to believe it will be revealed.

One of the sales teams I have had the pleasure to manage over my career has helped me to understand this. As a young salesman in a very competitive business, I once had a manager pull me into his office and tell me, "You do not impress me. In fact, I do not know why we even hired you. I don't believe you will ever make it in this business, so I'd like to give you some advice; when you are NOT here...you should be looking for alternative employment". I was enraged that anyone would talk to me like that. I venture to think that this manager was a genius or at least that he saw something in me and recognized how to ignite it. It's easier to think that, than the alternative that he was just being a jerk, and since then I will tell you I have come to appreciate the man who doesn't even necessarily recall who I am; only in passing. Years later, after some successes and failures I was "drafted" on to an All-Star sales team with the intent that someday I would lead them. They were a very solid group of veteran guys with incredible work ethic and insatiable drive as a TEAM; which is hard to find in sales.

My boss who hired me, in response to me asking him what the expectations were, said, "Just don't make me look stupid" for bringing me back into the company I had left several times before. How do you move the needle on an already successful team? What can I really bring to the table to help? I did my best to simply fit into the group and fall into my roles that I would naturally excel at. I learned under great leadership and did whatever I could to help my guys make as much money as they could. In my earlier years in the business the comment made to me by my current leader (which I consider a friend as well) could have railroaded my mentality. I feel the main reason it did not was I had already left this business multiple times and kept reengaging with it with fairly decent success. Therefore,

I knew I could be a formidable asset to the company.

Still, my focus turned from how any of the upper

management looked at me individually, and I began

focusing on my team and their incomes for their

families.

We began training on the basics, and during my

one-on-one meetings with them I began to "sharpen

their tools". I trained in how to read situations, and how

to better communicate and listen to customer's needs.

Then I recall having the conversations about their

incomes. As they told me where their incomes were, I

began to ask them why they would put the hours we put

in for that amount of money? I quickly realized they

needed a change in their mentality. I needed them to

know that they are worth more money because of what they do for their community and their customers. I am happy to report that after 6 years, with many obstacles, and a market that helped thrust us there; every single sales professional on my team increased their income significantly. We were able to help them realize their potential inside them. I will lose most of them to management opportunities, and perhaps even work for some of them. Still, this is what should happen when you realize your purpose; it's not only about you.

Never stop pursuing purpose. Whether it's your own, or if you are helping someone realize theirs. When I say that "we" were able to realize "their" potential; it is because sometimes it takes someone else's perspective to help you understand your worth. In this organization I've been blessed to be a part of the leaders who understand that if there is trouble the response is, "I am sorry, that was MY fault, I will take care of it", but when there is victory, the response is, "they did great, we have a great team, those guys are doing amazing". I feel very fortunate to have been able to see this in action in an organization. Once you realize that we are all, in our own way, facing the battlefield; we can begin to empathetically help those around us. Realize this, that while there are more defined individuals that may seem to have the upper hand early on in life; there are many more "Pawns" among us. Whereas the Rook can only do what a Rook can, and as the Knights, and Bishops locks into their abilities and patterns; slow and steady with deep unfulfilled and untapped purpose moves the Pawns into position in this game of life. The others will never know the feeling of being more than meets the eye, but the Pawn, if humbled in the hand of the chess master reaches the other side, soon will experience transformation. As it undergoes the move from Pawn to Queen, and all the ability and freedoms that come with it, the Pawn is soon to discover the purpose it has had within itself all along.

If you've made it this far, I want to say a simple "Thank You". My hope is that you have somehow gleaned some hope and encouragement from the words that you've read and found strength to engage life to the fullest.

Even more so, I would hope that this book has given perspective for allowing yourself to see amidst the people and situations that you encounter; the potential in the "pawns" of life.

In many cases the underlying value may not be immediately evident, so take your time to uncover and understand what you are seeing. When the moment hits you that you find yourself feeling less than worthy of the calling to better someone or something; find a mirror and look deep into your soul. Know that you have value and are able to make a difference. Wrapped up inside of you is the power to change your world.

I hope you are blessed!

Made in the USA
Columbia, SC
25 June 2024